SPORTS INJURIES:
HOW TO PREVENT, DIAGNOSE, & TREAT

FIELD HOCKEY

Sports Injuries:
How to Prevent, Diagnose, & Treat

- Baseball
- Basketball
- Cheerleading
- Equestrian
- Extreme Sports
- Field
- Field Hockey
- Football
- Gymnastics
- Hockey
- Ice Skating
- Lacrosse
- Soccer
- Track
- Volleyball
- Weight Training
- Wrestling

SPORTS INJURIES:
HOW TO PREVENT, DIAGNOSE, & TREAT

FIELD HOCKEY

VERONICA LEE

MASON CREST PUBLISHERS
www.masoncrest.com

Mason Crest Publishers Inc.
370 Reed Road
Broomall, PA 19008
(866) MCP-BOOK (toll free)
www.masoncrest.com

First printing

1 2 3 4 5 6 7 8 9 10

Library of Congress Cataloging-in-Publication Data on file
at the Library of Congress

ISBN 1-59084-631-1

Series ISBN 1-59084-625-7

Editorial and design by
Amber Books Ltd.
Bradley's Close
74–77 White Lion Street
London N1 9PF
www.amberbooks.co.uk

Project Editor: Michael Spilling
Design: Graham Curd
Picture Research: Natasha Jones

Printed and bound in the Hashemite Kingdom of Jordan

PICTURE CREDITS
Corbis: 6, 8, 10–11, 13, 14, 16, 18, 21, 22, 25, 27, 28, 30, 34, 36,
38, 39, 40, 43, 44, 47, 56, 58; ©**EMPICS**: 41, 52, 54, 57.

FRONT COVER: All ©EMPICS except Corbis (tr).

ILLUSTRATIONS: Courtesy of Amber Books except:
Bright Star Publishing plc: 45, 46, 48;
Tony Randell: 32.

CONTENTS

Foreword

Sports Injuries: How to Prevent, Diagnose, and Treat is a seventeen-volume series written for young people who are interested in learning about various sports and how to participate in them safely. Each volume examines the history of the sport and the rules of play; it also acts as a guide for prevention and treatment of injuries, and includes instruction on stretching, warming up, and strength training, all of which can help players avoid the most common musculoskeletal injuries. *Sports Injuries* offers ways for readers to improve their performance and gain more enjoyment from playing sports, and young athletes will find these volumes informative and helpful in their pursuit of excellence.

Sports medicine professionals assigned to a sport that they are not familiar with can also benefit from this series. For example, a football athletic trainer may need to provide medical care for a local gymnastics meet. Although the emergency medical principles and action plan would remain the same, the athletic trainer could provide better care for the gymnasts after reading a simple overview of the principles of gymnastics in *Sports Injuries*.

Although these books offer an overview, they are not intended to be comprehensive in the recognition and management of sports injuries. The text helps the reader appreciate and gain awareness of the common injuries possible during participation in sports. Reference material and directed readings are provided for those who want to delve further into the subject.

Written in a direct and easily accessible style, *Sports Injuries* is an enjoyable series that will help young people learn about sports and sports medicine.

Susan Saliba, Ph.D., National Athletic Trainers' Association Education Council

Defenders guard the goal line as the opposing team takes a corner at the 1991 U.S. Olympic Sports Festival.

History

Field hockey is one of the most popular games in the world. Games played with a ball and stick can be traced back more than four thousand years to the Nile Valley in Egypt, making it one of the world's oldest competitive team sports.

Indeed, field hockey is thought to be the forerunner of all "stick and ball" games, and such games have been played by civilizations across the world, from the Greeks and Romans to the Ethiopians and Aztecs. The modern game, however, evolved in England in the mid-nineteenth century. The British army subsequently introduced the game to India and throughout the British colonies, and, in 1895, the first international competition was held. It is perhaps for this reason that Great Britain, Australia, India, and Pakistan still dominate the sport at the international level.

The sport spread across the Atlantic in 1901, introduced by Constance Applebee, an English physical education instructor who was attending a seminar at Harvard University. The game received an enthusiastic response, and Applebee quickly spread the sport to some of the most prestigious schools in the United States, especially those in the Northeast. By 1922, the United States Field Hockey Association (USFHA) for women had been formed. The Field Hockey Association of America (FHAA) for men was formed in 1930. In 1924, the sport's international federation, the *Fédération Internationale de Hockey* (**FIH**) was formed.

Female students are seen here playing field hockey in front of the Albert Memorial in Kensington Gardens in London, England, in 1935.

The Olympic Games included men's field hockey on the official program for the first time in 1908, at the London games. Women's field hockey earned a spot on the program only in 1980, at the Moscow games. The sport's most coveted

Students take part in the first field hockey practice held at Smith College in Northampton, Massachusetts, in 1932. Note the long toes on their sticks, which look very outdated today.

international prize, however, is the World Cup, held every four years. The title is contended by sixteen men's and sixteen women's teams. The first men's title was won in 1971 and the first women's in 1974.

Now played in 132 countries, field hockey is the world's second most popular team sport after soccer. Generally, it is known simply as hockey. It is called field hockey in the United States and Canada simply to distinguish it from ice hockey.

RULES

Field hockey teams have eleven members—male or female, or, in recreational games, both. The object of the game is to score a greater number of goals than the opposition, and goals may be scored only from within the striking circle.

The game can be played indoors or outdoors, although the outdoor version is more widely played throughout the world. A game lasts for seventy minutes, divided into two halves of thirty-five minutes each. There is a five-to-ten-minute break between halves, and teams change ends at half time. In the event of an injury, play is suspended and the lost time is added on at the end of the second half.

Play is started by the team who wins the toss, and any other restart is determined by a **bully**. The team with the most goals at the end of the seventy minutes is the winner. It is also possible for a games to end in a draw (or a tie). But in some games—at a tournament, for example, or in a championship game—there must be a winner. In such cases, extra time is played, and the team to score first wins. If extra time does not produce a goal, the game ends with a penalty-stroke competition.

PITCH

A hockey field is 100 yards (91.5 m) long and 60 yards (54.9 m) wide. At each end is a goal, which is 7 feet (2.1 m) high and 4 yards (3.6 m) wide. A semicircular striking area—known as the circle, or striking circle—extends for a radius of 16 yards (14.6 m) around the goal. A penalty spot is marked 7 yards (6.4 m) into the circle from the center of the goal line. The stick has a flat, rounded face with a crooked end, which is often called the **toe**. Players may control and play the ball with the flat side of the stick only. This head must be made of wood, and the entire stick must weigh 12–28 ounces (340–790 g). The ball is made from a hard material (usually rubber), covered with a man-made material, such as PVC. It is usually white.

The Dartmouth College women's field hockey team plays a game against the University of Massachusetts in Amherst, Massachusetts, in 1995.

SURFACES

A hockey field may be covered with grass, all-weather material, or artificial turf, with either a sand or water base. There are practical advantages to using synthetic surfaces in hockey, and the number of artificial surfaces is increasing because they are easier and less costly to maintain. As a result, the International Hockey Federation has developed performance standards for hockey fields based on ball rebound, ball run and deviation, impact response, surface friction, dimensions, slope, smoothness, color, gloss, watering, porosity, and surface health.

Grass fields are high-maintenance and need a properly qualified groundskeeper to maintain, water, drain, reseed, and returf as necessary. Nonetheless, grass is by

The U.S. and Australia women's field hockey teams compete in the 1984 Summer Olympics, which were held in Los Angeles, California.

far the favored field for players. It "gives" more easily than artificial and man-made surfaces, meaning that players' joints and muscles are less easily jarred. The repeated stress of playing on hard surfaces can cause sore shins, stress fractures, and even **shin splints**. Natural grass, however, provides a cushioning effect, greater than synthetic turf, and is less stressful on the lower limbs because it absorbs ten percent more energy on impact than synthetic turf.

It is not surprising that players prefer grass fields. However, they must be well maintained—properly watered in hot months and properly drained in wet months. Ground that has been frozen over in winter or baked in summer will

INDOOR HOCKEY

Indoor hockey is a version of field hockey. It developed in Europe during the 1950s, mainly to enable serious hockey players to continue enjoying their sport through periods of bad winter weather. However, it is itself an exciting and enjoyable game and is now played around the world throughout the year.

The field is smaller than an outdoor field, measuring no bigger than 48 x 24 yards (44 x 22 m). Down the longer sidelines are boards that are 4 inches (10 cm) high to help keep the ball in play, creating a fast, flowing, exciting game.

Teams have only six players; and although players use the same equipment, they may only push the ball, not hit or flick it. Except for a shot on goal, the ball may be played only along the ground.

Each team has a goalkeeper, and the other five field players are dispersed over the playing field. No player has an exclusively defined role: The attackers are generally on attack and the defenders are generally on defense; but there are frequent exciting overlaps from defense into attack, and vice versa. A games lasts forty minutes, broken into two halves of twenty minutes each.

produce a surface so hard that players risk injury when hitting the ground—severe bruising, at least, and even fractures. Conversely, on a field that is too wet or muddy, players may not be able to stop and change direction effectively, causing ankle sprains and twisted knees.

Preparation to Avoid Injury

Why do sports players train? Not just to get physically fit, but to gain confidence. Many games are won by confidence, by believing that it is possible to win. Lose that confidence, and you lose the game. Train hard and develop your skills, and you will be able to step onto the field with a positive attitude.

Field hockey is a sport that requires players to have all-around conditioning. You must be able to endure periods of short sprints, with moderate to light runs in between. You need powerful leg strength for sprinting, as well as upper-body strength and power to perform explosive shots on goal and downfield passes. So, it is easy to see that you need to be fit to play hockey well. If you go into a game underprepared, you can easily lose or even get injured. Remember, an injury will have an impact not only on you, but also on your whole team. Your game strategy will be affected if the team loses a player—it may even cost your team the game. If your injury puts you out for the rest of the season, you will lose skills, and your performance will suffer when you finally return to the field.

Many people believe that a good mental attitude is as important as physical health in sports. Certainly, a positive attitude can make an ordinary team play beyond its capacity against a team of similar ability.

Dartmouth College women's team warms up before a game by practicing the various shots and maneuvers they will use over the following seventy minutes.

MENTAL PREPARATION

Before a game, prepare well. On the day itself, follow an appropriate warm-up routine and focus on the job ahead. Consider the weather conditions. Is it rainy? Is it sunny? Both of these will affect your game. The rain will make a grass field softer; hot sunshine means that you will need to drink more fluids throughout the game. Have you got all your equipment, and is it in good condition? Do you

Players warming up before a game practice their moves. Note the player on the right using reverse stick, as per the rules that only the flat side of the stick may be used to hit the ball.

have a game plan that all the team members understand? Do you feel ready to start playing?

At training sessions, listen to your coach. A coach will have much more experience than you do, and you can benefit from it. In particular, a good coach will be able to help you understand the sport: the best players can "read" a game, and adjust their play accordingly.

UNDERSTANDING THE GAME

Read as much about field hockey as you can—from training and technique to strategy. If you do not understand something that you read, ask your coach to explain it. If it can be demonstrated in a practice drill, go through the drill as many times as it takes for you to "get" the point.

Hockey may appear complex, but is in fact a simple game of attack and defense, and can easily be learned. There are two phases of the game: offense, or the attacking phase, when your team has the ball; and defense, or the defending phase, when your team's opponents have the ball.

In an attacking phase, the objectives are:

- to keep possession;
- to keep the ball moving forward, penetrating the defense at the earliest opportunity;
- to score goals.

In a defending phase, the objectives are:

- to regain possession at the earliest opportunity;
- to prevent the opposition from penetrating your own defense;
- to deprive the opposition of goal-scoring opportunities in your team's circle;
- to avoid giving up goals.

THE ABCs OF PASSING

You may be able to run with the ball and dodge tackles, but many coaches will agree that if you cannot pass, you cannot play. A pass involves two players—the passer and the receiver—working together.

There is no point in passing to a player who is not expecting it or who is surrounded by defenders. Look for a player standing alone. Even then, do not be too quick to pass; think of the possible outcome. Can the receiver make good use of this ball? Is the receiver running too fast or too slowly to reach the ball?

Effective passing depends on a number of simple but effective principles:

- the player must be AWARE of the positioning of teammates and opponents;
- the player must be BALANCED;
- the player must have CONTROL of the ball.

These are the ABCs of passing. Combined with knowing when to pass and when to hold onto the ball, this lets you "read" the game.

For each phase, different skills are required. Attacking requires players with composure, who can control the ball. This means having the ability to run with the ball, to pass and to receive a pass, and to create goal-scoring opportunities. Defending requires players with the ability to mark an opponent, to delay and close down opponents, to deny opponents' goal-making opportunities, and to protect and defend your goal.

On the team, no player other than the goalkeeper has a clearly defined role. The ten field players are spread out on the field and may play all over it. This means that, although field players can be put into one of three general categories—attackers, defenders, and midfielders—these categories do become blurred. Midfielders, in particular, are expected to offer both good defense and attack.

Two famed field hockey players, Kim Seung (left) and Nayak Dinesh, battle for the ball as South Korea and India meet in an international tournament.

Well-known field hockey player, Carole Thate, of the Netherlands, controls the ball as she runs with a reverse stick.

ATTACK

Control and composure are essential when players are attempting to retain possession, especially when you have opposing defenders intent on dispossessing you. While running, you must be able to maintain control over the ball and be aware of what is going on around you.

- Keep your body in as close to an upright position as possible, holding the stick at the top with the left hand. (Note that whether players are right- or left-handed, their grip of a stick is the same.)
- Both stick and ball should be kept out in front and slightly to the right of the body, making it easier to run fast and to look up to see where team players are on the field.
- Balanced footwork is essential to avoid tripping over your own feet, the ball, or the stick.
- Look ahead on the field to read the pattern of play and to know when to pass the ball, or when to keep it.

DEFENSE

Marking forms the basis of good defensive play. The primary aims of marking are to discourage passes, to force an error if a pass is made, or to tackle. There are three main methods of organizing a defense: one-on-one, zonal, and a combination of the two.

For one-on-one marking, when the opposing players have a ball, one defender marks an assigned opponent. This means staying as close as possible to the opponent, making it as difficult as possible for the opponent to receive a pass, and retaining a position between the opponent and the goal.

The aim of zonal marking is for defending players to form a zone as soon as possession is lost. Defenders take responsibility for any opponent who comes into their individual zone of defense. The zone concentrates and tightens marking in the area of greatest danger. Discipline and retaining organization are critical.

The most effective marking system uses a combination of both the zonal and

FIRST-AID KIT

The FIH has adopted a "no blood rule," which means that an injured player must leave the field after receiving an injury that causes bleeding. Players with bloodstains on body or clothing may not start or continue play. Wounds must be covered and the bleeding stopped before any player may reenter the game.

All clubs should have first aid materials on hand during practice sessions and games, including the following items:

- sealed sterile dressings
- band-aids
- elastic bandages
- sterile gauze pads
- adhesive tapes, safety pins
- plastic disposable gloves
- cleansing wipes
- scissors
- tweezers
- a blanket

In addition, a supply of clean water is advisable.

Argentine players compete in the Torneo de Reyes. Note how the goalkeeper's special equipment and body armor prevent her being hurt as players compete for the ball near her body.

the one-on-one marking systems. This relies on tight one-on-one marking of all opposition players immediately around a ball, with the cover defense using zonal marking outside of the vicinity of the ball.

The crucial moment for the team is when possession is lost. Failure to react quickly may enable the opposition to get more players into the danger area and to penetrate the shooting circle.

SHOTS IN YOUR ARMORY

Here are some terms that you might find useful when playing field hockey. There are six main types of pass used in the modern game. You should practice them all and learn in which situations to use them:

- Hit—used for passing the ball quickly over long distances, for shooting at the goal, and when taking free hits or hit-ins from the side and backline.
- Push—the most commonly used pass in the game. It lacks the speed of the hit, but is more accurate.
- Reverse push—most effective when passing from left to right over short distances, and when no open-stick pass is possible.
- Slap—similar to the push and used almost as often. The push is most effective over short distances, but the slap is used to make long, powerful, and penetrating passes.
- Flick—an extension of the push. Used to lift the ball into the air, either as a long overhead pass, or as a shot at goal over an opponent's stick or a fallen goalkeeper.
- Scoop—an alternative aerial pass, requiring an adjustment to the grip and body position. The foot and shoulder are brought forward to achieve the shoveling action that is needed to pass the ball high over an opponent.

A player prepares to take a free hit and uses a hit shot to pass the ball quickly over a long distance.

Warming Up to Prevent Injury

A proper warm-up is essential before playing any game. It is easy to neglect this stage of training, but players do so at the risk of pulling muscles or straining joints—injuries that may end a player's season.

A warm-up provides a smooth transition from rest to the intensity of competition, gradually raising both body temperature and heart rate. "Gradually" is the point: Even on warm summer days or indoors, players will wear warm clothing during the warm-up. For the same reason, players will put on warm clothing again at the end of play, when cooling down.

Warm-ups and stretching increase the muscle temperature, making muscles more elastic and flexible. This will also reduce the risk of injury by preventing the muscles from fatiguing easily. Another advantage of a warm-up is that it helps players to prepare psychologically before the games.

Every training exercise session or competition should start with a **cardiovascular** warm-up, which raises the pulse rate gradually to the level needed for strenuous activity. This can take various forms, such as easy cycling on an exercise bike, easy jogging, or skipping. This part of the warm-up usually takes five to ten minutes.

Players dribble the ball in a practice session. Practicing ball-handling skills is a vital component in your development as a field hockey player.

Warming up is vital before practice sessions and games. Here a player goes through some stretching exercises to loosen her hamstrings and lower back muscles.

STRETCHING

Stretching is the second phase of the warm-up, and there are two kinds of stretching:

- static—easy stretches that are held for ten to fifteen seconds, without straining;
- assisted—stretches using the help of your coach or training partner.

Static stretching should be related to the main activity. All field hockey players will stretch **hamstrings** and major muscles, but the goalkeeper will also want to do exercises of a more gymnastic nature to prepare for the repeated diving and falling that is likely during a game.

When stretching, start at the top (with the neck and shoulder) and work down to the feet and ankles, paying particular attention to the lower back, calves, and ankles. Stretch gently and slowly—hold each position for fifteen to twenty seconds. Try to keep your breathing slow and easy; it is all too easy to hold your breath as you stretch.

Lower back

Field hockey players are prone to sore muscles in the lower back because of the amount of bending they do during games. Therefore, pay particular attention to stretching this region. Simple exercises, such as sitting on the floor and trying to touch your toes, or standing and trying to touch your toes, are very effective. But never force a stretch or exercise—ease yourself into it.

Shin splints

If you have suffered shin splints in the past or are playing on artificial surfaces, you should remember two things: The shin muscle actually works against the large calf muscles, and it is the last muscle to warm up and the first to cool down. With this in mind, make sure that your warm-up routine includes exercises to strengthen this muscle—for example, flexing the foot away from the leg, and rising up and down on the balls of your feet.

To stretch your neck, face forward and move your head slowly from side to side, moving your right ear as close as is comfortable to your right shoulder. Repeat on your left. Face forward again, turn your face as far to the right as you can without straining, then to the left. Finally, with face forward once more, move your head down to your chest, then as far back as you can without straining.

Calf muscles

The calf muscle is, in fact, two muscles. The gastrocnemius muscle originates above the knee, and is therefore best stretched when the knee is straight. The soleus muscle originates below the knee and is best stretched with a bent knee.

To stretch the gastrocnemius, first keep the heel of the one leg on the ground. Step well forward with the other leg, then lean forward until you feel a stretch on the straight back leg.

To stretch the soleus, first place one foot flat on a chair. Use your hands to push your bent knee forward until the muscle starts to feel a little tight.

Hamstrings

To stretch the hamstrings, sit on the floor with your legs in front of you, then flex your feet and bring the toes toward your shin. This will stretch the hamstrings and also maintain good calf flexibility.

Ankles

Ankle injuries are very common for field hockey

To stretch your quadriceps (the large muscles at the front of the thigh), stand on one leg, then lift the other leg and grasp it at the ankle with one hand to flex the knee joint. Hold for ten seconds, then repeat with the other leg.

Stretch your hamstrings by sitting on the floor with your legs in front of you, then flex your feet and bring your toes toward your shin.

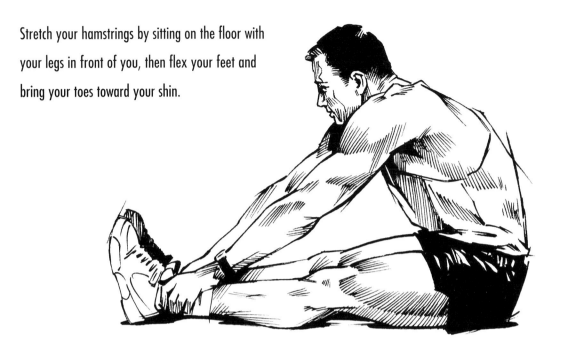

players, so pay particular attention to warming up the ankles. Simple rotation exercises are very useful—for example, make circles with your feet.

Finish your warm-up with some fast sprints over short distances. The warm-up should be timed so that your team finishes just before going on the field.

THE COOL-DOWN

Every training session and game should end with a cool-down. A cool-down gradually returns your body to its normal temperature and your pulse rate to the resting level. This helps to prevent stiffness and soreness in the muscles by dispersing lactic acid. You should put your warm clothing back on for cool-down, which should take ten to fifteen minutes.

Repeat the same activities as for a warm-up, but hold the static stretches slightly longer—about thirty to thirty-five seconds.

Equipment

Field hockey is a noncontact sport, which means that players need to wear very little protective gear. But as you play at more competitive levels, you will notice that the pace of the game becomes faster, and therefore the risk of injury increases.

At a more competitive level, you should wear gloves to protect your fingers and shinguards to protect your shins. Some players also choose to use a mouth guard to protect their teeth; these should be properly fitted. Goalkeepers, of course, should wear a helmet and face guard during training and competition.

The most important items of equipment, however, are your boots and stick. Always ask for professional advice when buying these.

Measure your feet, making sure you are wearing your normal sports socks. Find out whether most of your games will be on natural or on artificial surfaces, and buy appropriate cleats and studs. Some boots have detachable cleats or studs so that you may change them according to the surface you are playing on. If you buy boots with permanent cleats or studs, you will need different boots for different surfaces.

Hockey sticks used to be made entirely from hard wood, but are now usually composed of hard wood that is wrapped and reinforced by such protective materials as carbon, fiberglass, or ceramic. These add strength and durability to the stick, while also giving a flexibility that minimizes injury to players' wrists and arm muscles.

A goalkeeper makes herself "as big as possible" when protecting the goal from a penalty shot. Note that she is wearing full protective gear and is holding her stick in one hand, to give maximum range of movement.

Two players go for the ball. Note the different stances of the attacking player (right) and the defending player (left) and that the defensive player is gaining more length (or reach) by holding the stick just in one hand.

A flexible stick that absorbs shock is often the stick of choice for beginning or novice players. Flexible sticks tend to be more durable than their stiffer counterparts. Advanced players, however, may choose a stiffer stick for increased power. Manufacturers may add a variety of reinforcing materials to the stick to add strength and durability or to promote either stiffness or flexibility. Fully composite and fiberglass sticks are legal at the collegiate and high-school level; revised definitions of the stick at the international level allow the stick to "be made of or contain wood or any material other than metal or metallic components, provided it is fit for the purpose of playing hockey and is no risk to health."

When choosing a field hockey stick, remember that its length and weight should be right for your height and strength. If the stick is the wrong weight for your age and size, you may damage your wrists, and you will not be in full control of your play. If your stick is too short, you can hurt your back by having to lean forward and down unnecessarily. If the stick is too long, you will find it hard to control the ball. Another consideration is that sticks come with different types of toes (see box below).

PROTECTIVE EQUIPMENT

Shin guards are a wise investment for field hockey players; they protect your shins from accidental hits by sticks and offer a sort of shock absorption from even a fast-moving ball. They come in various lengths and girths, and you should try different sizes and shapes to see which fits best. Some shin guards come with ties

TOES

There are many different kinds of toes, according to your needs:

- **Shorti—A popular toe size for attack players as well as younger players, the shorter toe enables a player to turn the stick over the ball faster.**
- **Midi—A midi toe offers a greater surface area for receiving passes than a shorti, yet is still compact enough to allow easy transition to the reverse stick.**
- **Hook—Designed primarily for defenders, a hook has a large surface area for tackling and stopping passes. It is also good for deeper grass and for uneven terrain where balls may bounce over a shorter toe.**

STICK LENGTH

Stick length is chosen based on a player's height. When choosing a stick, select the longest one that you can comfortably control. The more skilled you are, the longer the stick you will be able to handle.

PLAYER'S HEIGHT	STICK LENGTH
Up to 5 ft	34 in (86 cm)
5 ft–5 ft 3 in	35 in (89 cm)
5 ft 3 in–5 ft 7 in	36 in (91 cm)
5 ft 8 in–5 ft 11 in	37 in (94 cm)
Over 5 ft 11 in	38 in (97 cm)

In field hockey, goalkeepers prefer a shorter and lighter stick than field players because they play with their stick in one hand. Forwards prefer a lighter stick for quick maneuvering in the circle, while defenders often choose a heavier stick for powerful clearing hits and to prevent attackers from casually "pushing" the stick aside.

Joining sticks just before a game starts is a good way to remind all squad members that teamwork is vital.

A goalkeeper skillfully stops the ball between stick and shin guards while in a sliding motion.

or straps; others are made without either and fit neatly down the front of your socks. Choose whichever feels most comfortable.

If you use a mouth guard, make sure that it is measured and fitted by an orthodontist. As your teeth develop, you will need to replace your mouth guard; this is something your orthodontist can help you with. Never share a mouth guard—this is unhygienic and may damage the natural development of your teeth.

Serious eye injuries are rare, but players are more frequently choosing to wear goggles to protect their eyes. Make sure your goggles give you the best all-round vision possible.

Weather permitting, most field hockey players wear short-sleeved shirts and shorts or skirts. If you play on artificial surfaces, you may want to wear long-sleeved tops and track pants to minimize friction burns if you should fall.

MAINTAINING YOUR EQUIPMENT

Take care of your protective equipment, and it will take care of you, saving you from painful injury.

- After playing, let your equipment air out, so that perspiration can dry naturally.
- Wipe off all moisture and mud before you pack anything away in your sports bag.
- Replace mouth guards at the first sign of wear (cracks or splits).
- Store all equipment as recommended by the manufacturer.

Marcin Pobuta of Poland uses a typical goalkeeper's one-handed swing to bring down the ball (and then kick it clear of the shooting circle) after a shot by an opponent.

Field players need only minimal protective equipment. For goalkeepers, it is a different matter: They face fiercely hit shots on goal, including penalties, and may use any part of their body to stop, but not hold, a shot. For this reason, goalkeepers pad or protect as much of their body as possible.

Goalkeeping equipment must be shock-absorbent so that injuries are minimized and also lightweight so that it does not weigh down the goalkeeper too much or greatly restrict move-ment. There is a wide range of equipment available, but the following pieces are recommended for goalkeepers:

• helmet and strong visor;
• throat protector;
• chest pad;
• gloves;
• abdominal protector;
• athletic protector;
• padded shorts and thigh protectors;
• lightweight leg guards;
• knee pads;
• boots.

Germany's Britta Becker in action during the Olympic qualifying tournament in 2000.

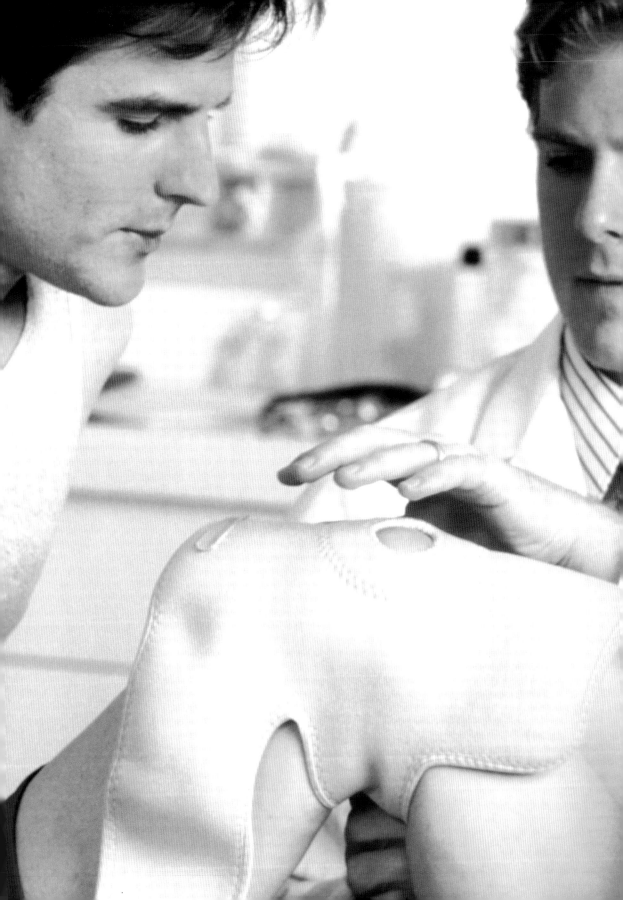

Common Injuries and Treatment

Physical contact is not allowed in field hockey, and players may not push, shove, charge, strike, or handle an opponent in an attempt to play the ball. But in a fast-paced sport with sticks and balls, contact injuries can and do occur.

The first thing to remember is to play safely and with consideration. Do not, for example, raise your stick above shoulder height, and do not hit the ball dangerously high. Playing by these and other hockey rules may prevent injury to you, a member of your team, or a member of the opposing team.

Fitness and a proper warm-up are also important for preventing injuries. Tight muscles are more likely to be strained, and players with an injury from which they have not fully recovered are more likely to be re-injured. Previous ankle and knee injuries that have healed may still require extra support, but taping or bracing should never be used to enable you to play while you are injured.

About 75 percent of injuries in field hockey are caused when a player is struck by either the ball or a stick. As for the other 25 percent, this is a game that requires players to accelerate quickly and execute rapid changes of direction, so most of these can be attributed to such movements. Relatively few injuries occur as a result of contact with another player.

A medical doctor fits an individually made knee protector for a field hockey player. It gives support to the joint, yet allows the player to be mobile during recuperation after an injury.

A medical doctor explains what she sees on an X-ray to an injured athlete. Never be tempted to start playing again before your doctor or physical therapist says that your injury is healed.

The most common injuries are sprains and strains, bruising and **lacerations**, and fractures. These occur mainly to the upper limbs, namely, the hand and forearm; the lower limbs, namely, the ankle, foot, and knee; and the face, mostly after being struck by the stick or ball—but remember that injuries to the eyes and teeth are infrequent. Overuse injuries to the ankles and lower back are also common. Such injuries, also called chronic injuries, come from performing the same action over and over.

Abrasions to the legs, particularly the knees, and to the arms, particularly the elbows, are more common on artificial surfaces. Joint injuries are also more common on artificial surfaces because the field has less "give." Indeed, anecdotal evidence suggests that ankle sprains and the prevalence of shin soreness, knee pain, and lower-back problems have increased with the more widespread use of synthetic surfaces. The abrasive nature of synthetic playing surfaces has meant that lacerations are more frequent as well. Artificial fields can also cause friction burns when a player slides or falls on them. The knees and arms, in particular, are affected.

FOREARM

The forearm is particularly prone to bruising from a hockey stick or ball during a game.

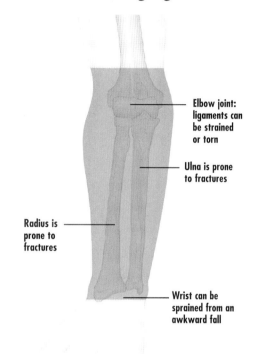

Elbow joint: ligaments can be strained or torn

Ulna is prone to fractures

Radius is prone to fractures

Wrist can be sprained from an awkward fall

INJURIES CAUSED BY THE STICK AND BALL

In hockey, the ball can reach speeds of up to 80 miles per hour (128 km/h), which may mean serious injury if a player is hit. With the exception of the goalkeeper, field hockey players wear little protective clothing and are vulnerable to blows on any part of the body. Field players may not stop or control the ball with anything other than the flat side of their stick, so they must take the blow of a ball they cannot stop with their stick, or else they will forfeit a free hit, a **penalty corner**, or even a penalty stroke.

The penalty corner is usually the most dangerous phase of play for ball injuries because it involves defenders rushing out of the goal area toward an attacker who is hitting the ball as hard as possible toward the goal. Bruising or fractures are common. Players may also be struck by a stick when they are in close contact with another player. There are rules penalizing dangerous play—such as raising a stick above shoulder height—but accidental blows do occur.

HAMSTRINGS

Hamstring injuries and strains can immobilize athletes for extended periods.

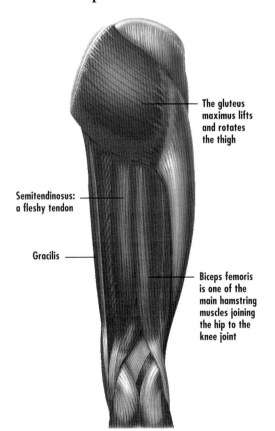

The gluteus maximus lifts and rotates the thigh

Semitendinosus: a fleshy tendon

Gracilis

Biceps femoris is one of the main hamstring muscles joining the hip to the knee joint

The majority of finger wounds are caused by being hit by the ball or an opponent's stick. Most finger injuries are suffered during a bully or when defending a penalty corner, when defenders may be rushing off the goal line toward a ball struck hard by an attacker. To help prevent these kinds of injuries, wear gloves, have good stick discipline, and know where the ball is at all times.

As with any fast-moving game that requires rapid acceleration and changes in direction, field hockey can cause various injuries to the muscles and joints. Typical are pulled hamstrings and groin muscles, which occur during rapid acceleration; and sprained ankles and knee **ligament** injuries, caused during a rapid change of direction. Dislocations of the knee can also occur if the knee is struck while in a flexed (bent) position.

Ankle strains probably account for the greatest loss of playing time of any injury, but they can be prevented by improving ankle stability. Incorporate flexibility and strength exercises in preseason training. To prevent recurrent ankle injuries, ensure full recovery of ankle function before returning to play.

Field hockey is a rough and tumble game. Here, U.S. player Cindy Werley falls as Kim Myung-Ok (left) and Jeon Young-Sun of South Korea challenge for the ball during the 1996 Olympics.

INJURIES CAUSED BY THE PLAYING SURFACE

An uneven playing surface can cause the ball's movements to be unpredictable, and it may fly up after hitting a bump. Uneven surfaces also increase the risk of sprained joints, particularly the knee and ankle, with associated damage to **cartilage** and ligaments in the case of the knee.

The field should be inspected before each half for damage. Grass fields should be inspected for loose divots, which can cause ankle sprains and make the ball roll unpredictably. Artificial fields should be inspected for wear and tear.

Artificial surfaces can be hard on joints and muscles, and some field hockey players who play entirely on artificial surfaces may experience shin splints. Physiologically, these are an inflammation of the tendons or muscle in the shin area. Symptoms include swelling, lumps, and redness over the hardness of the shin, and the most common cause is overuse or running on hard surfaces.

Splints may also develop if you run with your weight too far forward or wear ill-fitting boots. Remember, too, that the shin muscle works against the

SHIN MUSCLES

It is important to strengthen the shin muscle, which works against the large calf muscles.

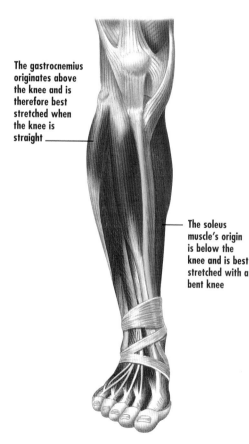

The gastrocnemius originates above the knee and is therefore best stretched when the knee is straight

The soleus muscle's origin is below the knee and is best stretched with a bent knee

WHAT TO DO IN CASE OF AN INJURY

TALK—Ask the player what happened. Where does it hurt? What kind of pain is it?

OBSERVE—Check the affected area for redness or swelling. Is the injured side different from the other side?

TOUCH—Touch can help you assess pain; warmth will indicate that the area is inflamed.

ACTIVE MOVEMENT—Ask the injured player to move the injured part without any help.

PASSIVE MOVEMENT—If the player cannot move the injured part, carefully try to move it yourself through its full range of motion.

SKILL TEST—Did both the active and passive movement produce pain? If not, ask the player first to stand, and then to demonstrate hockey skills.

If an injury is identified, remove the player from the activity immediately. Note, too, that the above guidelines do not apply when assessing head injuries or concussion, or for a suspected spinal injury. In the case of a suspected spinal injury, keep the player lying flat and immobile until professional medical help is available.

large calf muscles, so if you fail to warm up, these muscles may be tight, causing problems. If you suffer from shin splints, you will feel pain when extending the toes and when putting weight on the injured leg. It will also hurt if you press the area with your finger. The pain will ease when you are well warmed up, but resume at

TREATING MINOR INJURIES

Nose bleeds

These are caused by being hit by a stick or ball.

- Have the player sit down with his head forward.
- Loosen any tight clothing around the neck and chest.
- Tell the player to pinch the nostrils firmly at the soft part of the nose for ten minutes and to breathe through the mouth. If bleeding continues after this, reapply pressure.
- Advise the player to spit out any blood in the mouth, because it may cause nausea.
- If bleeding has not stopped after thirty minutes of continuous pressure, call for an ambulance.
- Do not use nose plugs.

Bruises

Ask yourself:

- Has the force applied by stick or ball been hard enough to cause internal injury?
- Is there loss of function of the part affected?
- Is there any tenderness on the bone in the area?
- Does the player have any signs of being in shock?

If the answer to any of these questions is yes, seek professional medical help. Otherwise, follow the R.I.C.E. procedure.

the end of exercise. To prevent shin splints, incorporate flexibility exercises in your training. To treat, follow the R.I.C.E. program (see below), alternating ice packs with moist heat.

THE R.I.C.E. PROGRAM

For any injury, players should seek prompt attention from a professional with first-aid qualifications. Also, follow the **R.I.C.E.** program, which stands for "rest, ice, compression, and elevation." This method of treatment is believed to reduce the possibility of further damage to injured soft tissue by reducing swelling in the area.

Rest

Rest reduces further damage—stop activity as soon as the injury occurs. Avoid as much movement as possible to limit further injury and do not put any weight on the injured part of the body.

Ice

Ice cools the tissue and reduces pain, swelling, and bleeding. Place ice wrapped in a damp towel on the injured area—never directly on bare skin— and hold the ice pack firmly in place with a bandage. Repeat the ice treatment for twenty minutes every two hours during the first forty-eight hour period.

Compression

Compression also helps to reduce bleeding and swelling. Use a **compression bandage**. Be sure that the bandage is not so tight that it cuts off circulation or causes tingling or pain to the area outside the bandage, and always bandage the injury between ice treatments.

Field hockey is a fast-moving sport and injuries can and do occur on the field of play. When this happens, the R.I.C.E procedure should be followed.

Elevation

Elevation helps to stop bleeding and reduce swelling. As much as possible, keep the injured area raised; use a pillow for comfort and support.

Consult a medical professional, such as a doctor or physical therapist, if you are worried about the injury, or if the pain or swelling worsens. Seek treatment if the pain or swelling has not gone down significantly within forty-eight hours.

REHABILITATION

The next step is rehabilitation. A player must be fully recovered before returning to play, as a premature return may make the injury worse and result in more time off the field. The time frame for rehabilitation and return to play may vary, depending on the nature and severity of the injury. Always seek the advice of a medical professional and follow a rehabilitation program that is specific to you and your injury. If you suffer from a recurring joint injury, seek professional advice about preventive bracing of the joint.

OVERUSE INJURIES

An overuse, or chronic, injury is caused by repeating the same action many times. This is not as serious as an acute injury, but any chronic problem may become worse if not acknowledged early on, so players should seek medical advice and treatment. Overuse injuries have both mental and physical symptoms:

- unusual tiredness or fatigue
- feeling very emotional, particularly depressed, anxious, or stressed
- a lack of appetite
- an inability to sleep at night
- muscle soreness and cramps
- stiff, painful, or unstable joints
- problems getting parts of the body comfortable in bed at night
- painful tendons
- pain that shows no improvement for more than three days

Taking Your Game Further

Field hockey is what is known as a "niche" sport in the United States. Although gaining in popularity, it is played mostly in the northeastern states and California, by only about 100,000 people. There are no full-time professional leagues, but it is possible to work as a team coach in high school or college.

For more information, contact the United States Field Hockey Association (**USFHA**), the sport's governing body in the United States. The organization currently seeks to foster and develop the amateur sport of field hockey by providing participation opportunities for players, coaches, officials, and administrators, and by preparing teams to represent the United States in international competitions.

Nearly 14,000 players, coaches, officials, and fans enjoy the benefits of USFHA membership, which costs ten to fifteen dollars for juniors, depending on age. As the sport's national governing body, recognized by the International Hockey Federation (FIH) and the United States Olympic Committee (USOC), USFHA is responsible for the training and selection of the United States teams for international competitions, including the Olympic Games, Pan-American Games, and World Cup.

Field hockey is such an exciting sport that you might want to make a career of it. To do this, you can become a high school or college coach.

A happy team captain holds a trophy when her team wins a youth tournament in Pisa, Italy. Field hockey is a sport played on all five continents.

HOCKEY CAMPS

The USFHA conducts clinics, camps, exhibitions, and professional-development programs to provide for the growth of the sport while providing continuing education to established players, coaches, and umpires. Currently, USFHA operates partner camps in twenty-three states with the aim of uncovering young talent and developing it right through to Olympic-participation level. Promising athletes of high-school age are invited to participate in training camps and tournaments to prepare for possible future international competition on one of the elite national squads.

The college and high school open camps of USFHA are held each summer as part of the association's commitment to developing the game. Separate high school and collegiate camps enable individual players to improve skills, tactics, and strategies.

As part of its mission, USFHA seeks to develop the sport while strengthening the idea of field hockey as a lifetime activity. It works toward this goal by partnering with community-based sports organizations—such as the local Parks and Recreation Department, YMCA, YWCA, and Boys and Girls Clubs—to

India's Baljeet Singh (left) and South Korea's Seung-Jin You show how competitive field hockey can be during the 1996 Olympic Games in Atlanta, Georgia.

A group of high school field hockey players from Washington High School in Princess Anne, Maryland, takes a break from practice.

increase public awareness of the game, to provide program continuity, and to pool administrative, coaching, and umpiring resources, offering better support for players at the local level. Regional and youth coordinators work to introduce the sport in communities where field hockey is not an established activity, while also providing support in communities with a tradition of playing the game.

If you are going on to college and want to continue playing there, or if you hope to apply for a field hockey scholarship, contact the National Collegiate Athletic Association (NCAA). They can tell you if your chosen college has a field hockey program, and if it offers field hockey scholarships and participation in collegiate leagues. Whichever way you hope to continue with this fine and exhilarating sport, play well and play safely.

USFHA MISSION STATEMENT

As its mission, USFHA seeks to:

- **Foster and develop the amateur sport of field hockey.**
- **Provide participation and development opportunities for players, coaches, officials, and administrators.**
- **Prepare teams to participate in the Olympic Games, Pan-American Games, and other USOC-sponsored events, as well as international competitions sponsored by the FIH and other national governing bodies.**
- **Represent the United States internationally and domestically by serving as ambassadors of goodwill and setting a standard of excellence in playing, coaching, officiating, and administrating.**

Glossary

Abrasion: An injury caused when the top layers of skin are rubbed or scraped away.

Bully: A means of restarting the game. Facing one another, and with the ball between them, two opponents strike the ground and then the other's stick three times, and then may play the ball.

Cardiovascular: "Cardiovascular exercise" is any exercise that improves the health and function of the heart and lungs.

Cartilage: Strong connective tissue found in the body's joints and other structures. Children have a higher percentage of cartilage than adults, some of which turns to bone as they grow older.

Compression bandage: A bandage that holds a swollen joint or muscle tightly to reduce the swelling.

Field player: Any member of the team except the goalkeeper. Without a clearly defined role, field players may run all over the field, and may find themselves playing both attack and defense in a single game.

FIH: Abbreviation for the *Fédération Internationale de Hockey*, the sport's international governing body.

Hamstrings: The group of three muscles set at the back of the thigh.

Laceration: A jagged wound caused by rough tearing or cutting.

Ligament: A short band of tough body tissue, which connects bones or holds together joints.

Penalty corner: A hit awarded to an attacking player from any point on the goal line not less than 10 yards (9 m) from the nearest goalpost. Corners are awarded when the defense fouls in its own circle.

Reverse stick: Inverting the hockey stick by twisting the wrists to sharply change the direction of the ball.

R.I.C.E.: An injury treatment program of rest, ice, compression, and elevation.

R.O.M.: Abbrevation for Range of Motion, which may describe exercises designed to restore full flexibility to a damaged joint or muscle.

Shin splints: The common name for medial tibial stress syndrome, which causes pain at the front of the lower leg.

Toe: The crooked end of the stick, which has a flat, rounded face.

USFHA: Abbreviation for the United States Field Hockey Association, the sport's national governing body.

Further Information

USEFUL WEB SITES

Fédération Internationale de Hockey (FIH): www.fihockey.org

The National Collegiate Athletic Association (NCAA): www.ncaa.org

United States Field Hockey Association (USFHA): www.usfieldhockey.com

The Web sites listed on this page were active at the time of publication. The publisher is not responsible for Web sites that have changed their address or discontinued operation since the date of publication. The publisher will review and update the Web sites upon each reprint.

FURTHER READING

Adelson, Bruce. *The Composite Guide to Field Hockey*. Broomall, Pennsylvania: Chelsea House Publishers, 2000.

Anders, Elizabeth and Sue Myers. *Field Hockey: Steps to Success*. Champaign, Illinois: Human Kinetics, 1999.

Axton, William F. and Wendy Lee Martin. *Field Hockey*. Indianapolis, Indiana: McGraw-Hill, 1993.

Keegan, Thomas. *College Bound Student-Athlete Guide to Field Hockey*. Toronto, Ontario: Hushion House, 2002.

_____*Prep School Field Hockey Guide*. Flagler Beach, Florida: Athletic Guide Publishing, 2002.

Marx, Josef and Gunter Wagner. *Field Hockey Training for Young Players: Introducing the Game to Young Players*. Aachen, Germany: Meyer & Meyer Sports, 2000.

THE AUTHOR

Veronica Lee is a journalist and author who was born and educated in London, England. As a cultural commentator and sports writer, she contributes regularly to several British newspapers, including *The Observer*, where she is also chief copy editor of the "Sport" section. Veronica played field hockey throughout her school and college career, competing to county level, and maintains a keen interest in the sport.

THE CONSULTANTS

Susan Saliba, Ph.D., is a senior associate athletic trainer and a clinical instructor at the University of Virginia in Charlottesville, Virginia. A certified athletic trainer and licensed physical therapist, Dr. Saliba provides sports medicine care, including prevention, treatment, and rehabilitation for the varsity athletes at the University. Dr. Saliba holds dual appointments as an Assistant Professor in the Curry School of Education and the Department of Orthopaedic Surgery. She is a member of the National Athletic Trainers' Association's Educational Executive Committee and its Clinical Education Committee.

Eric Small, M.D., a Harvard-trained sports medicine physician, is a nationally recognized expert in the field of sports injuries, nutritional supplements, and weight management programs. He is author of *Kids & Sports* (2002) and is Assistant Clinical Professor of Pediatrics, Orthopedics, and Rehabilitation Medicine at Mount Sinai School of Medicine in New York. He is also Director of the Sports Medicine Center for Young Athletes at Blythedale Children's Hospital in Valhalla, New York. Dr. Small has served on the American Academy of Pediatrics Committee on Sports Medicine for the past six years, where he develops national policy regarding children's medical issues and sports.

Index